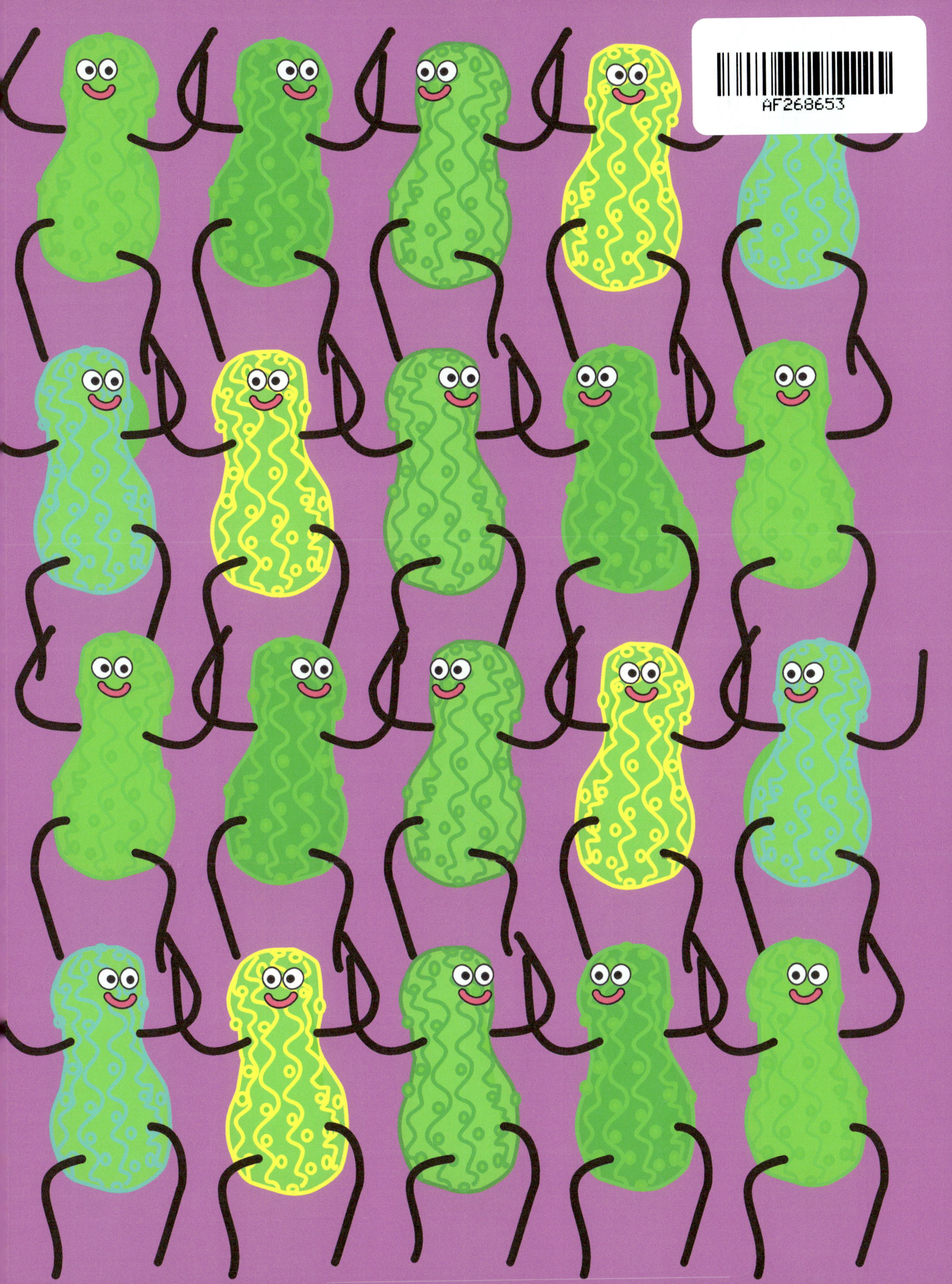
AF268653

BIG GRATITUDE

To my family and friends for all the Love and support
and for always making me laugh!

Many thanks to CJ for not getting frustrated at
my learning curve and for putting so many things together
for me!

For my blessings,
(that I dont count often enough)

To the
Big Guy Upstairs,
Thanks for EVERYTHING!!!

LOVE THE WORLD,
Heather New

About the Author
Heather New

I am an artist living in Canada,
and my biggest joy comes from
my family and friends.
I Love music and art,but most of all,
I Love being silly and laughing!

I spent years volunteering as a clown,
and especially loved
painting the faces of children
from all cultures, races
and backgrounds.

I have attained worldwide attention
for engraving motorcycles,and now
I have decided to try something new
by writing a children's book.

It is my hope that we will all look
for common ground
with those we perceive to be
different from ourselves.

Wouldn't it be a great world
if we could figure out a way to be friends
with everyone ?

P.S.
Look for the 4-leaf clovers! They are everywhere!
You only need to discover them....

This is a pickle.
His name is Ace.
He likes to smear ice cream
all over his face.

This is a pickle.
Her name is Bernice.
She goes to the park,
and dances with geese.

This is a pickle.
His name is Cliffy.
He'll fix your rocking chair
in a jiffy.
No,ye canny shuv yer granny off a bus
GLUE

This is a pickle.
His name is Doug.
A grasshopper is his
favourite bug.

I promise
I'll
change!

I'm
free
!!!

Run
Auntie
run!

I'm your
Uncle.

This is a pickle.
His name is Ed.
He puts cheese slices
upon his head.

This is a pickle.
His name is Frank.
He wears a disguise
when he goes to the bank.

This is a pickle.
His name is Guy.
He squirted citrus juice
into his eye.
ORANGE you glad we didn't get your other eye?
My Eye! Owie Owie Owie!
When life gives you lemons, make lemonade!
Limey! that's got to sting!

This is a pickle.
Her name is Heather.
She Loves to tap dance
in rainy weather.
Tippity Tap
Tippity Tap

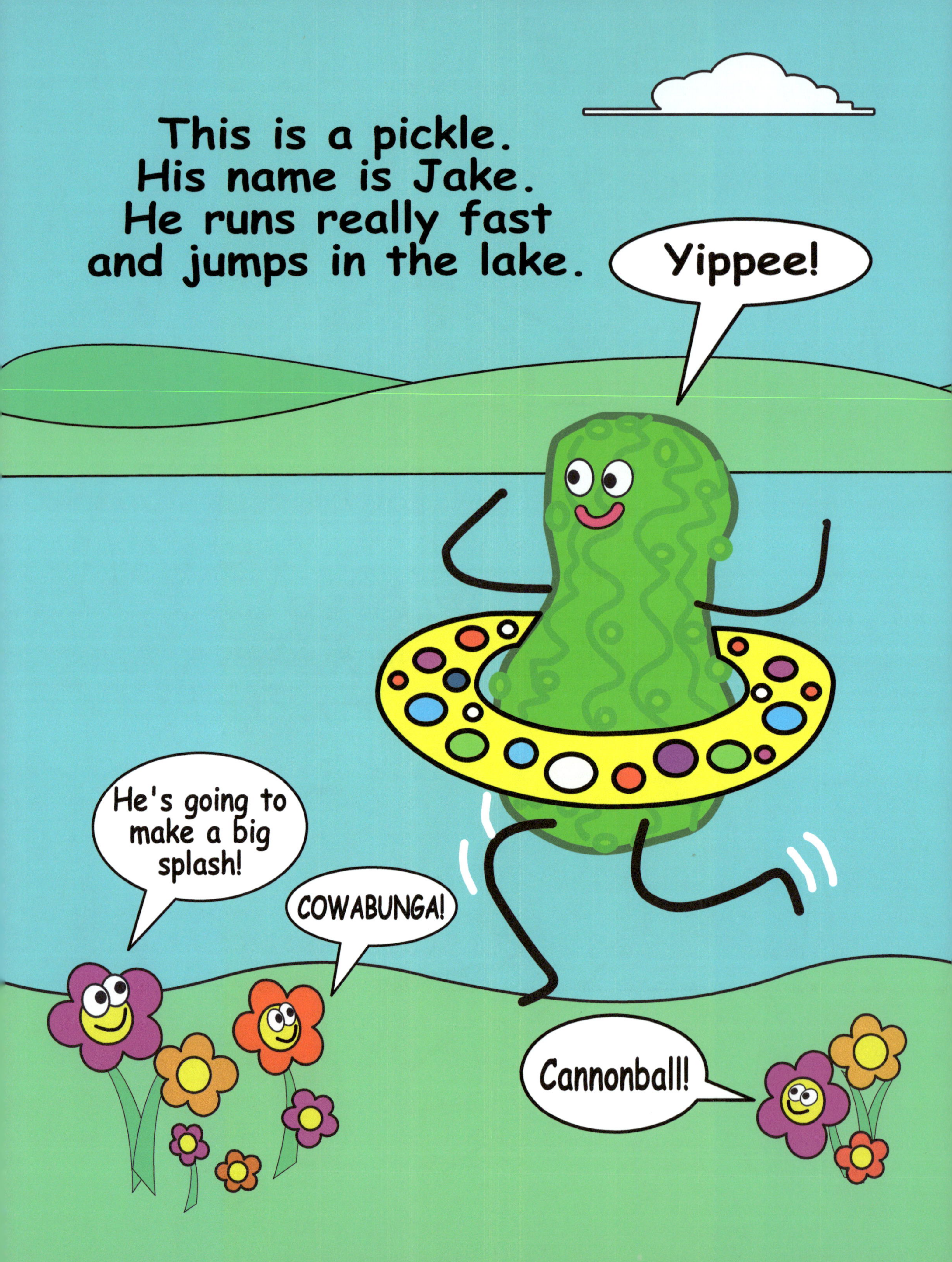

This is a pickle.
His name is Jake.
He runs really fast
and jumps in the lake.
Yippee!
He's going to make a big splash!
COWABUNGA!
Cannonball!

This is a pickle.
Her name is Kiki.
She has a pineapple
who can be rather squeaky.
SQUEAK
SQUEAK
SQUEAK
ENOUGH
with the
SQUEAKING!
I'd squeak too,
but I'm all
CLAMMED up.!

This is a pickle.
His name is Louie.
He plays with gunk
that is slimy and gooey.

This is a pickle.
His name is Moe.
He yells really loud
when he stubs his toe.

This is a pickle. His name is Noah.
His nose gets itchy from his pet boa.

This is a pickle.
Her name is Patty.
Her teacher says
she is much too chatty.
Blah blah blah
blah blah
blah blah blah
A
B
C

This is a pickle.
Her name is Odette.
She's cleaning the kitchen,
but isn't done yet.

This is a pickle.
His name is Quinn.
He runs up the stairs,
then runs down again.
Hey!
It sounds like a
thunderstorm
up there !

This is a pickle.
Her name is Roxanne.
She swings from the curtains
just like Tarzan.

This is a pickle.
His name is Steve.
He always spills gravy
onto his sleeve.

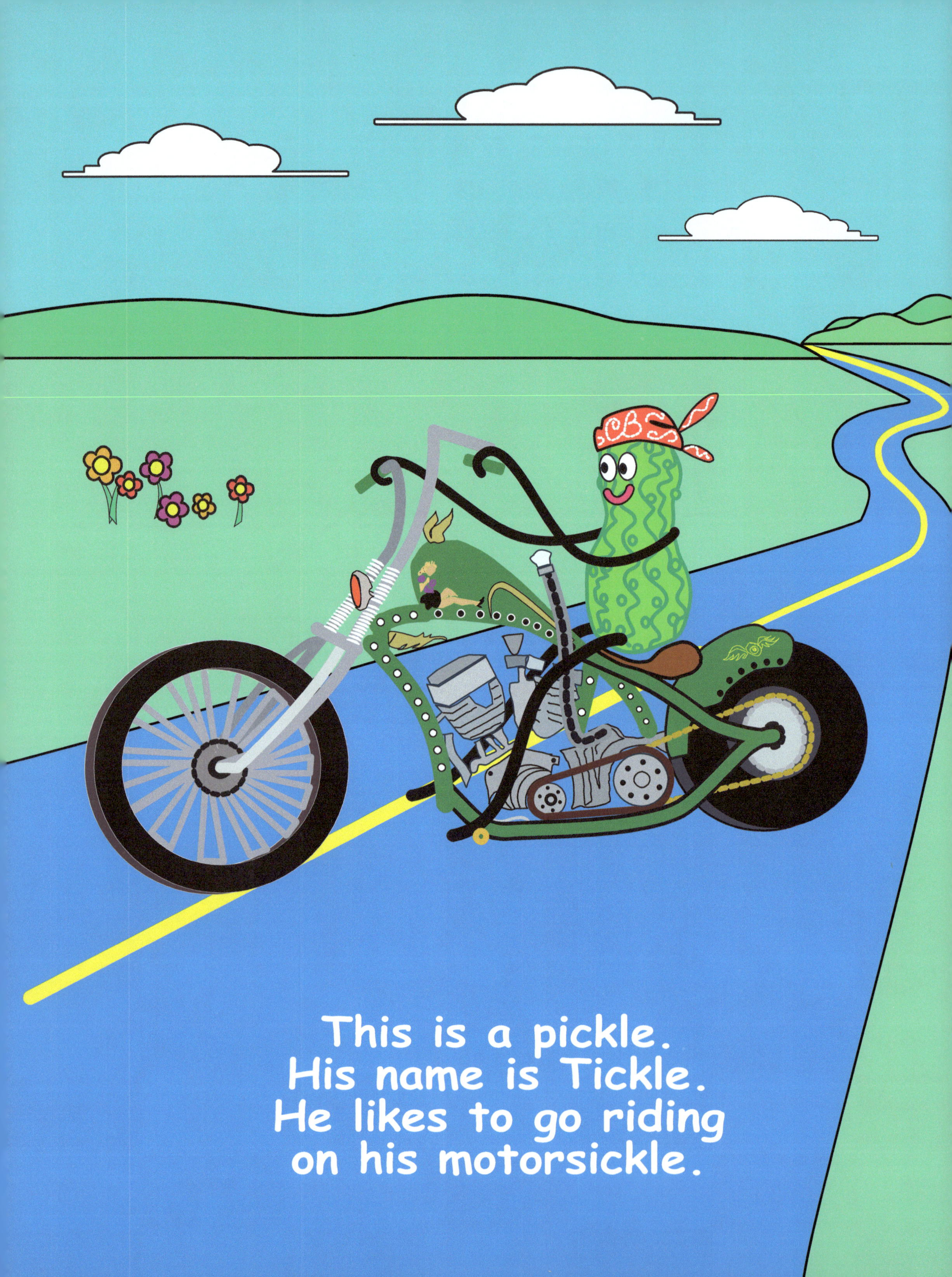

This is a pickle.
His name is Tickle.
He likes to go riding
on his motorsickle.

This is a pickle.
His name is Uriah.
He plays groovy tunes
with his friend, Papaya.

burp
burp
burp
burp
This is a pickle.
Her name is Viola.
She gets the hiccups
when she drinks cola.
burp
burp
burp
burp
burp
burp
burp
burp
burp
burp
burp
burp
burp
burp
burp
burp
burp
Hiccup
BURP
Hiccup
COLA
Hiccup
It is polite
to say
"excuse me"
!!!

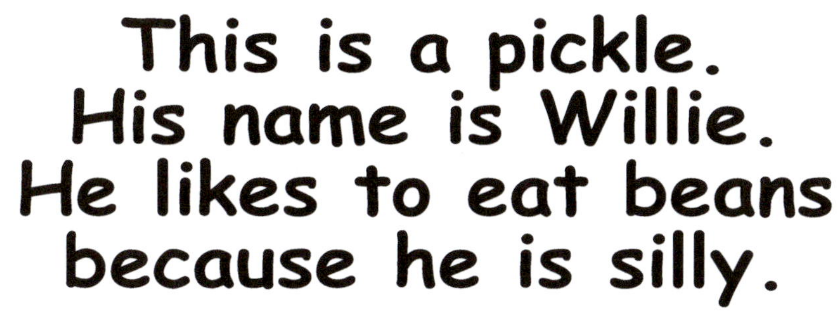

This is a pickle.
His name is Willie.
He likes to eat beans
because he is silly.

BEANS
I smell natural gas!

This is a pickle.
His name is Xavier.
He gets extra dessert
for perfect behaviour.

This is a pickle.
His name is Yuri.
His bathrobe is warm
and his slippers are furry.

This is a pickle.
His name is Zeke.
He likes to go fishing
down by the creek.

Whether
your name
starts with
an A,B or C,
remember
you're
awesome
like pickle
and me!

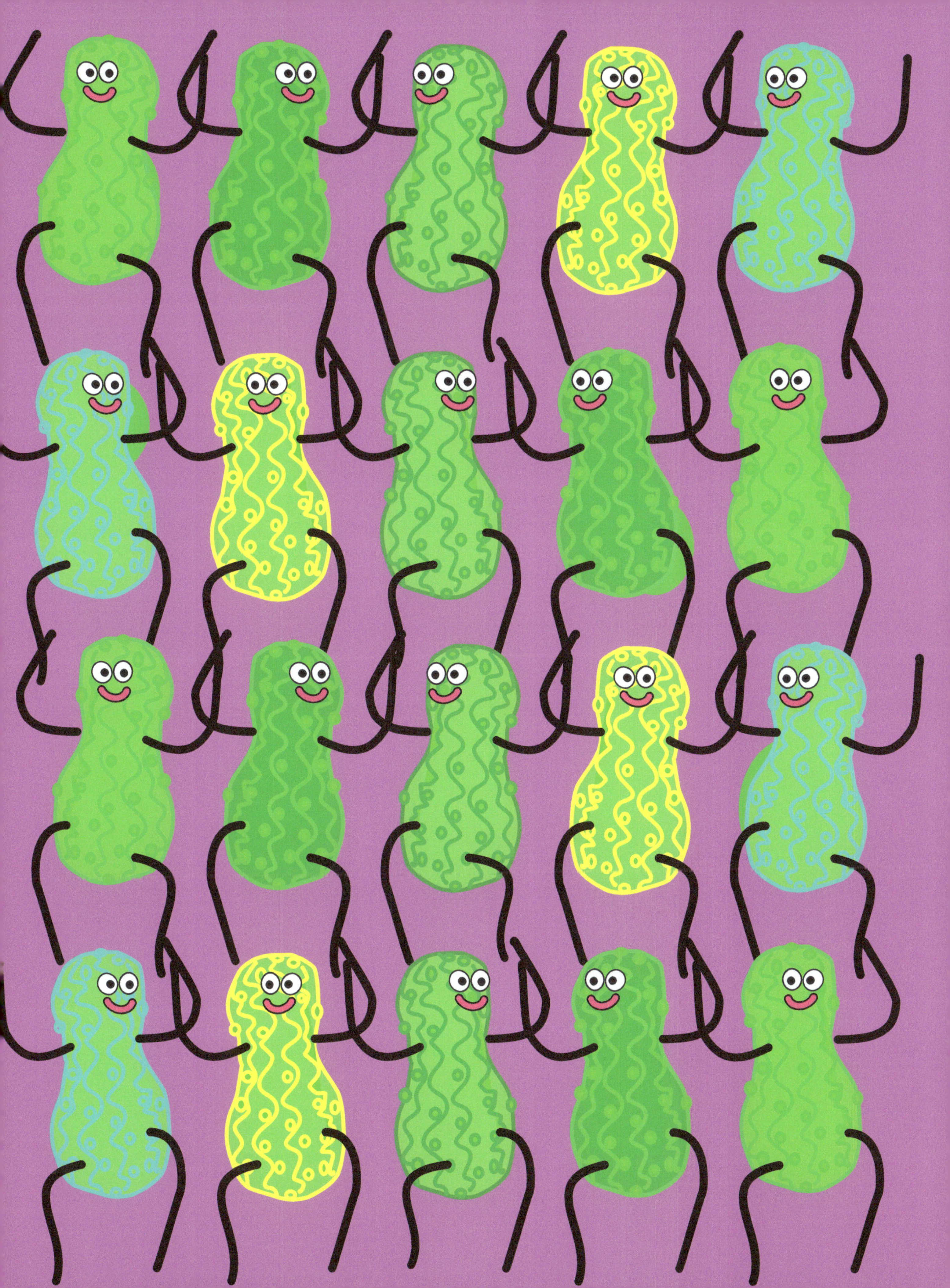

Draw and colour a pickle
doing your favourite thing!

Send your art to
Heather New Children's Books
on Facebook and Instagram !